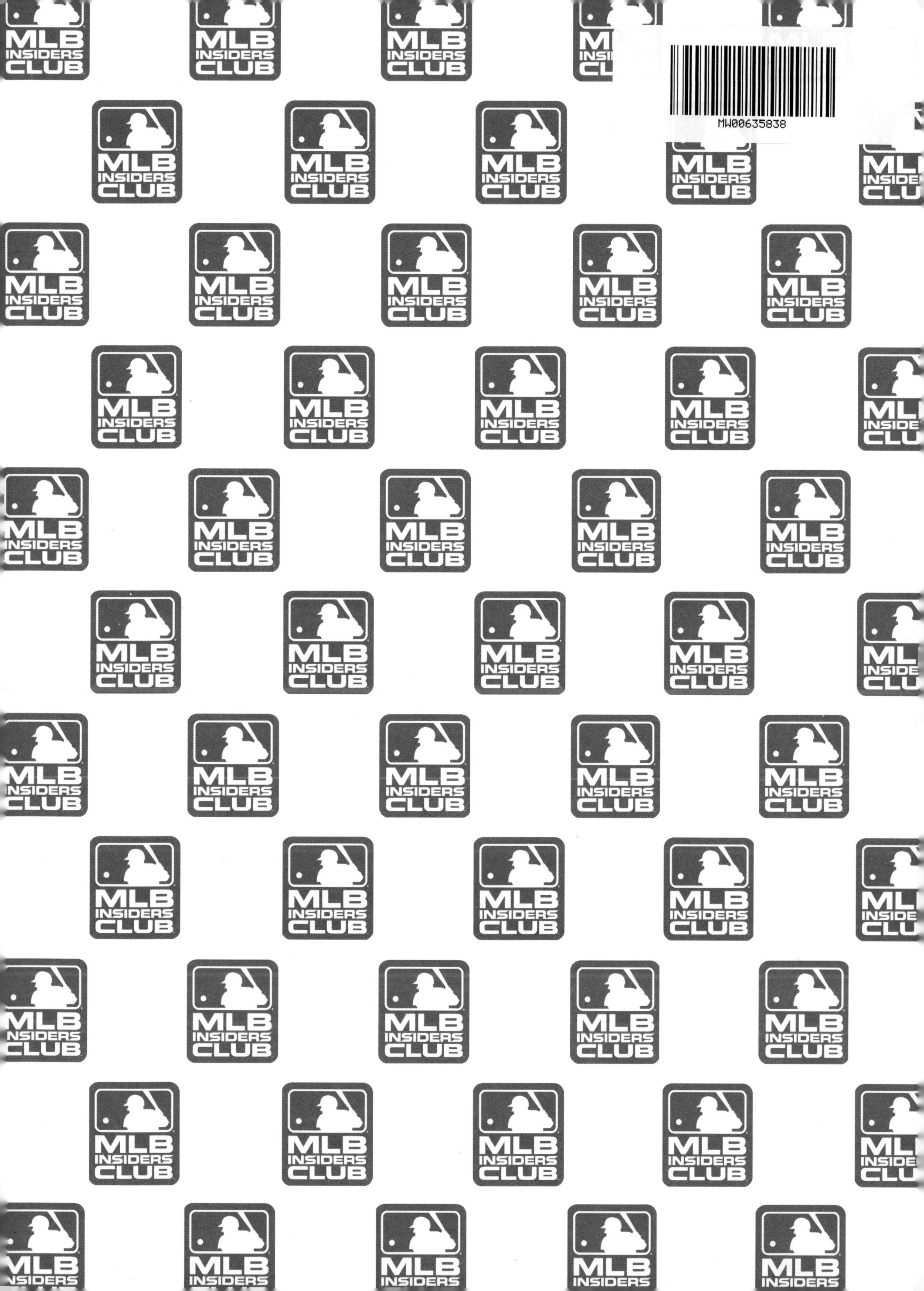
MLB INSIDERS CLUB
MW00635838

Batter's Eye
A Photographic View of Our National Pastime
Amtrak.com
Gulf
mazda
superguarantee on superpages.com
DELTA
freecreditreport.com
BUD LIGHT
371
LINCOLN
37 14 41 42 SHEA
MLB INSIDERS CLUB
Baseball Insiders Library

NYY 0 NY 0
Visit Amtrak.com
Visit Amtrak.com
167
65

Batter's Eye

A Photographic View of Our National Pastime

MLB INSIDERS CLUB

Baseball Insiders Library®

BATTER'S EYE

A Photographic View of Our National Pastime

Printed in 2011

ACKNOWLEDGEMENTS

Major League Baseball would like to thank Pat Kelly and Milo Stewart Jr. at the National Baseball Hall of Fame and Museum for their invaluable assistance, as well as Eric Enders for his diligent work in helping to prepare the book for publication.

Vice President, Publishing
Donald S. Hintze

Editorial Director
Mike McCormick

Publications Art Director
Faith M. Rittenberg

Senior Production Manager
Claire Walsh

Managing Editor
Jon Schwartz

Associate Art Director
Melanie Finnern

Senior Publishing Coordinator
Anamika Panchoo

Project Assistant Editors
Allison Duffy, Chris Greenberg, Jake Schwartzstein

Editorial Interns
Nick Carroll, Bill San Antonio

Director
Rich Pilling

Photo Editor
Jessica Foster

Assistant Photo Editor
Charlotte Brown

MLB INSIDERS CLUB

Managing Editor
Jen Weaverling

Art Director
Brian Peterson

Proofreader
Travis Bullinger

2 3 4 5 6 7 8 9 10 / 12 11

ISBN: 978-1-58159-534-5

MLB Insiders Club
12301 Whitewater Drive
Minnetonka, MN 55343

Table of Contents

24

Introduction

If a picture is truly worth 1,000 words, as the oft-quoted adage states, then this collection of photographs from more than a century of Major League Baseball history may contain more passion, joy, humor and drama than most of the weighty hardball tomes at your local library. Within these pages are iconic images of a young Ty Cobb fearlessly sliding into third base at Hilltop Park in New York in 1909, Willie Mays sprinting deep, deep, deep into right-center field at the Polo Grounds to make "The Catch" in the 1954 Fall Classic and an upside-down Ozzie Smith midway through an exuberant back-flip celebration.

Of course, the inherent beauty of the national pastime is not just found in the select moments that have become ingrained in the larger culture. Each trip to the ballpark offers myriad tiny miracles, from the way the setting sun tinges the sky in the early innings of an evening game and the geometric beauty of a perfectly executed bunt to the intimate interaction of fathers and sons in the stands — and sometimes in the dugout. All of these singular, fleeting moments have been etched into the individual memories of fans and players over the decades, and occasionally a photographer has been on hand to snap some of them so that they can be enjoyed by the rest of us. *Batter's Eye* collects many of these photographic keepsakes to be cherished and passed along from one generation to the next like heirlooms.

Ca
TOYOTA
VERLÄNDER
35
JENKS
45
2

maraderie

AT&T PARK
SAN FRANCISCO
GIANTS
TOYOTA
SAFEWAY
Budweiser
10
13
VAN SLYK
18
55

Previous spread: American League All-Stars cheer on their teammates during the 78th Midsummer Classic at AT&T Park in San Francisco. The AL defeated the NL, 5-4. Opposite page: Fathers and sons have been bonding over the game of baseball for more than a century. Most have played catch together in their backyards or at local diamonds. Ken Griffey Sr. (right) and his son, Ken Griffey Jr., were lucky enough to share a dugout, and occasionally the outfield, with the Seattle Mariners in 1990 and 1991.

Camaraderie

Opposite page: Cleveland Indians teammates Steve Gromek (left) and Larry Doby embrace after Game 4 of the 1948 World Series, a watershed moment for the newly integrated sport.
Above: Dustin Pedroia and the Boston Red Sox gather at the dugout rail during the 2009 American League Division Series.

While Big League teammates often try to boost each other's confidence during the season, sometimes — as Rod Carew shows a Minnesota Twins teammate — it's just as important to burst the bubble of one flying too high.

Camaraderie

Staying loose is one of those baseball cliches that is supposed to help a team during the long season. Torii Hunter (left) and Chone Figgins led by example for the 2009 Los Angeles Angels.

Camaraderie

Camaraderie

Arguably the most skilled hitter ever to swing a baseball bat, Boston Red Sox icon Ted Williams generously shared his philosophies with fans and teammates alike. In fact, the guarded Williams, seen here during Spring Training in 1956, was perhaps more at ease talking about his trade than any other subject.

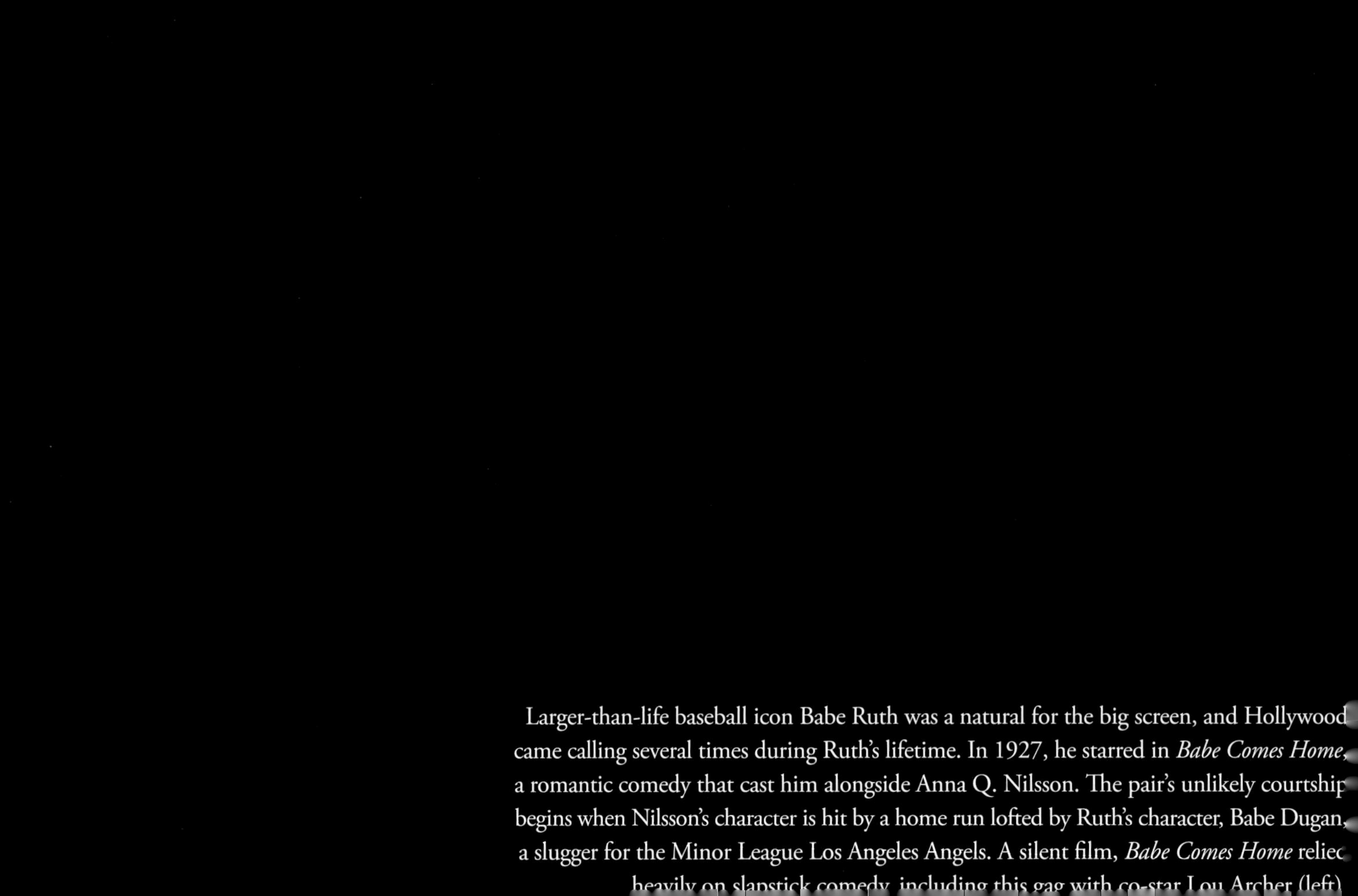

Larger-than-life baseball icon Babe Ruth was a natural for the big screen, and Hollywood came calling several times during Ruth's lifetime. In 1927, he starred in *Babe Comes Home*, a romantic comedy that cast him alongside Anna Q. Nilsson. The pair's unlikely courtship begins when Nilsson's character is hit by a home run lofted by Ruth's character, Babe Dugan, a slugger for the Minor League Los Angeles Angels. A silent film, *Babe Comes Home* relied heavily on slapstick comedy, including this gag with co-star Lou Archer (left).

A

Nicknamed "the Beast" for having a muscular build during the 1920s and '30s when most ballplayers were bantamweights, Philadelphia A's slugger Jimmie Foxx proved to be a gentle giant when it came to his young fans.

Camaraderie

13' 18"

Elements

Amtrak.com
Gulf
mazda
superguarantee on superpages.com
37
14
41
42
SHEA
DELTA
freecreditreport.com
BUD LIGHT
371
LINCOLN

General Motors
FOUNTAIN
16
6
American League
National League
40
42

Elements

Previous spread: Red sky at night, Citi Field delight.
Opposite page: A rainbow cuts through the haze over Detroit's Comerica Park during a 2003 Interleague tilt.
Above: A rainbow heralds the end of a rain delay at Chicago's Wrigley Field in 2008.

Although Opening Day is considered an annual rite of spring, Matt Lawton and the Cleveland Indians battled the snow — as well as the Baltimore Orioles — at Camden Yards in Baltimore to begin the 2003 campaign.

The clouds above Wrigley Field in Chicago roll back to reveal the setting sun.

Elements

Even when a hard rain falls at Nationals Park in Washington, D.C., fans brave the drops and remain glued to the action.

Elements

FENWAY PARK
P 1 2 3 4 5 6 7 8 9 10 R H E P
28 TOR AUGUST 22
11 BOSTON
25 SEA
52 NYY
58
35
51

Elements

Opposite page: As a cloudburst sends fans and players for cover, the grounds crew at Fenway Park is a frenzied blur of activity. Above: Just because the game is on hold during a rain delay at U.S. Cellular Field in 2005 doesn't mean that players, like the Chicago White Sox's Willie Harris, can't make a splash.

Rain at Petco Park in San Diego — seen pooling on a plexiglass stairway cover — is a rare occurrence.

Element

As packed as Boston's intimate Fenway Park can feel during Red Sox games, few things can clear out the stands better than a sudden burst of rain.

Element

Hardware
Hardware

TPX
GENUINE C271S
MAGGLIO ORDONEZ
DETROIT TIGERS

Intensity

Intensity

Previous spread: Each game is meaningful when a team takes the field — as the Colorado Rockies did here.
Opposite page: As a manager and a player, Lou Piniella breathed fire throughout nearly five decades in baseball.
Above left: New York Mets shortstop Rafael Santana stalks the field at Shea Stadium during the '86 Series.
Above right: Middle reliever Santiago Casilla doesn't take a single out for granted as the San Francisco Giants march to the 2010 World Series.

BALL
STRIKE OUT
RED SOX

Boston Red Sox left fielder Jason Bay doesn't lose focus as he tracks a fly ball to Fenway Park's Green Monster in 2009.

Intensit

New York Mets high-octane shortstop Jose Reyes is nearly on his way to first base before dropping down a bunt.

REYES
7

Intensity

Opposite page: Los Angeles Angels center fielder Torii Hunter earned the nickname "Spider-man" for his proficiency at scaling walls. Above: As a rookie in 2010, Atlanta Braves outfielder Jason Heyward possessed a degree of poise and power that belied his youth.

Rickey Henderson's blazing speed and relentless will to win established him as an all-time great during his career, which included 14 seasons with the Oakland A's.

Intensity

A's
330

Intensity

37

Intensity

By playing with grit during his 20 years with the Milwaukee Brewers, Robin Yount (sliding into Ken Oberkfell of the St. Louis Cardinals) forged a Hall-of-Fame career.

With each headfirst slide into third base, every superlative defensive play at shortstop and every laser-like home run, the Colorado Rockies can be sure that they have a franchise cornerstone in Troy Tulowitzki.

Intensity

KSM

Intensity

Opposite page: Cincinnati Reds catcher Johnny Bench has his eyes on the prize during the 1972 World Series. Above: Reds second baseman Brandon Phillips stretches himself to the limit but comes up inches short.

Intensity

Baseball is a game of angles and timing, and the Arizona D-backs' Augie Ojeda drops a perfectly placed bunt to utilize both.

Intensity

Opposite page: St. Louis Cardinals ace Bob Gibson unleashes a pitch from his overpowering arsenal in 1973.
Above: Fans at Yankee Stadium watch expectantly as Brooklyn Dodgers pitcher Russ Meyer delivers during the 1955 World Series.

Intensity

Opposite page: David Bell sacrifices some lumber in a bid for a hit for the Philadelphia Phillies.
Above: Boston Red Sox leadoff man Jacoby Ellsbury squeaks across a run as the New York Yankees' Joba Chamberlain fields a late throw.

Ballparks

AT&T PARK

3
5
5

Previous spread: McCovey Cove is an idyllic backdrop to San Francisco's AT&T Park. This spread: The ivy enveloping the outfield wall at Wrigley Field was first planted in 1937.

Ballpark

Fenway Park's Green Monster is an imposing yet iconic structure.

TRIKE OUT
Ballpark

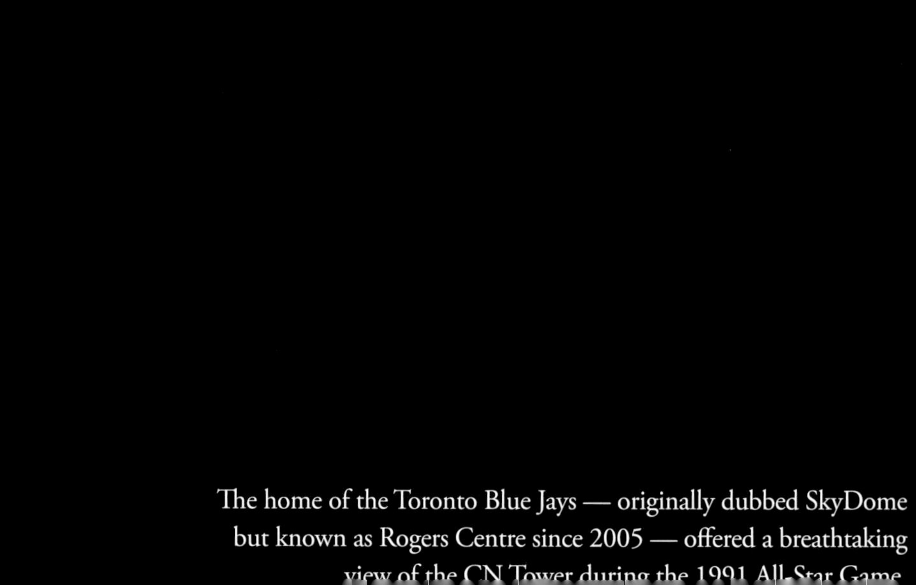

The home of the Toronto Blue Jays — originally dubbed SkyDome but known as Rogers Centre since 2005 — offered a breathtaking view of the CN Tower during the 1991 All-Star Game.

THE SUN
Bud
LEGG MASON
Coca-Cola
UNIVERSITY
OF MARYLAND MEDICINE
allfirst

Ballparks

Opposite page: The B&O Warehouse spanning right field helps make Oriole Park at Camden Yards one the most unique ballparks in the Majors.
Above: Fans descend on Coors Field from Denver's LoDo District.

Ballparks

Even with support beams obstructing views from certain seats, few parks were ever as beloved as Tiger Stadium.

By the time the All-Star Game returned to old Yankee Stadium (left) in 2008, the Bronx's next baseball cathedral was already rising.

Ballpark

Classics

IRATES
21

Previous spread: The always graceful Roberto Clemente slides into third base.
This spread: By consistently winning with class, Derek Jeter has etched his name among New York Yankees legends.

Classics

Tearing into third base in a blur of dirt and spikes, the Detroit Tigers' Ty Cobb was the game's fiercest player in its early years.

Classics

Opposite page: President John F. Kennedy got the Washington Senators' 1963 season underway with a ceremonial toss. Above: Camden Yards was a fount of jubilation and admiration on the night that Baltimore Orioles legend Cal Ripken Jr. eclipsed Lou Gehrig's consecutive-games-played streak in 1995.

Although he had already earned the nickname "Charlie Hustle" earlier in his career, Cincinnati Reds rally starter Pete Rose dove into third base in 1975 as if he maniacally needed to prove his mettle.

With his wholesome looks, dogged work ethic and devastating fastball, right-handed pitcher Tom Seaver transformed the New York Mets from the National League's court jesters in the mid 1960s to steely-eyed title contenders by 1969.

In one of sport's most poignant moments, Lou Gehrig delivered his "Luckiest Man" farewell speech on July 4, 1939.

42

As New York Giants outfielder Bobby Thomson crossed home plate after hitting the
"Shot Heard 'Round the World" at the Polo Grounds in 1951, he ignited a celebration
throughout Manhattan. As the party began, the Brooklyn Dodgers' Jackie Robinson

Classics

College-aged fans gathered atop the Cathedral of Learning on the campus of the University of Pittsburgh to root on the Pirates at nearby Forbes Field during Game 7 of the 1960 World Series.

Classics

President Barack Obama took in the Opening Day festivities at Nationals Park in Washington, D.C., in 2010.

Classics

Opposite page: Remembered simply as "The Catch," Willie Mays' signature over-the-shoulder grab in Game 1 of the 1954 World Series propelled the New York Giants to the championship. Above: Reporters and TV cameras crowded around Philadelphia Phillies pitcher Roy Halladay in 2010 after he authored a no-hitter in the first playoff start of his career.

After spending the entire offseason just one longball behind Babe Ruth's career record, Atlanta Braves icon Hank Aaron launched one over the left-field fence at Atlanta-Fulton County Stadium on April 8, 1974, placing him atop the all-time career home run list.

OFFICIAL WATCH
LONGINES
AT BAT 44
BALL 1
STRIKE 0
OUT 0
PLAY SCORING
LOS ANGELES
ATLANTA
DODGERS

24
Classics

In a rare moment of solitude, the San Francisco Giants' five-tool superstar, Willie Mays, heads for the home clubhouse.

Classics

at 8:18 CDT on Sept. 8, 1998, as Mark
McGwire hit his 62nd homer of the seaso

With a young fan looking on, Vice President Richard Nixon threw out the ceremonial first pitch at a 1959 Washington Senators game at Griffith Stadium.

Enjoying his final Bronx homecoming on the 25th anniversary of the ballpark that he was so often credited with building, New York Yankees icon Babe Ruth appeared before the fans at Yankee Stadium on June 13, 1948. He died two months later.

Ente
Phil

rtainment

Previous spread: Few mascots have a more adoring fanbase than the Phillie Phanatic.
This spread: St. Louis Cardinals legend Ozzie Smith's "Wizard of Oz" persona was as much a result of his signature backflips as his similarly acrobatic defensive mastery.

Entertainmen

Entertainment

Just as likely to wax poetic as he is to crack a joke, Ichiro Suzuki knows how to command the attention of media around the globe.

A statue of Johnny Bench outside Great American Ball Park in Cincinnati allows a new generation to embrace Reds history.

Entertainment

Southpaw, the Chicago White Sox's mascot, considers moonlighting as a photographer.

Entertainment

A young employee adjusting the manual scoreboard at Griffith Stadium in Washington, D.C., had a one-of-a-kind vantage point for every Washington Senators home game

ON. 0 1 0 0
SH. 5 0 0 0

Entertainment

Opposite page: Typically reserved, Ted Williams, the Boston Red Sox's batting king, didn't shy away from this movie camera.
Above: Often caught on the other side of the lens during his rise to stardom with the Oakland A's, Barry Zito uses a medium format camera during a Spring Training photo shoot in 2005.

Entertainment

AT&T Park in San Francisco offers fans of all ages the chance to glimpse the action free of charge behind the right-field wall.

Entertainment

Opposite page: Even St. Louis Cardinals mascot Fredbird has a pregame routine before he's ready for action.
Above: A trio of young New York Mets supporters are enthralled by their heroes, who took the field for the inaugural Opening Day game at Shea Stadium in 1964.

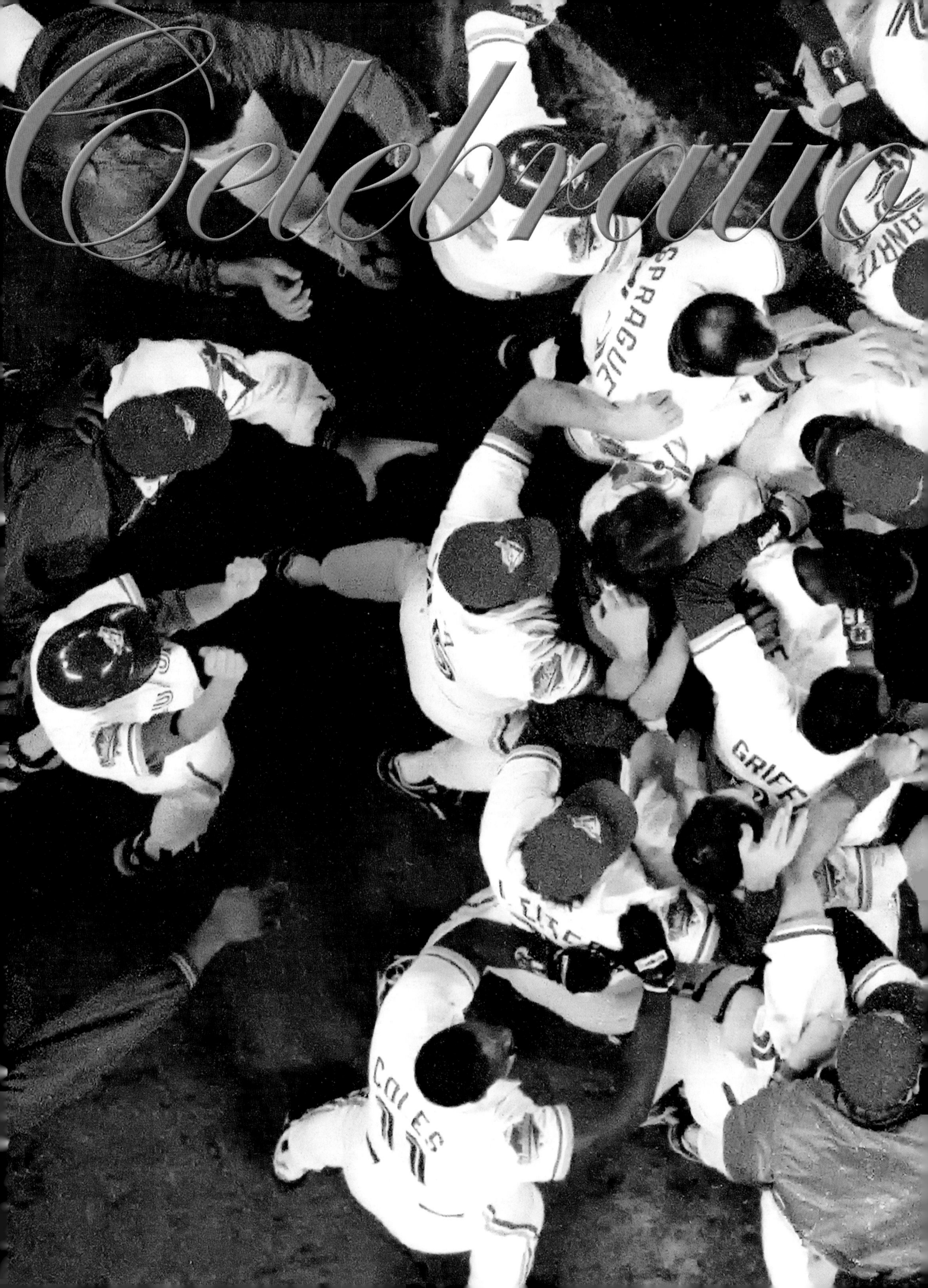
Celebratio
SPRAGUE
GRIFF
COLES

Previous spread: Victorious Toronto Blue Jays players clamor around 1993 World Series hero Joe Carter.
This spread: Clinching the AL pennant at home in Arlington in 2010 makes the Texas Rangers' first-ever trip to the Fall Classic in franchise history even sweeter.

Celebration

Celebration

Opposite page: New York Yankees Manager Joe Torre lets his emotions show after his team captures the 2000 World Series. Above: The Minnesota Twins swarm slugger Jim Thome after a walk-off homer in 2010.

An eruption of pride — and fireworks — fill the night at Edison Field as the 2002 Los Angeles Angels win the first World Series crown in franchise history. The title was clinched in a winner-take-all Game 7 victory over the San Francisco Giants.

Celebration

13
FOX

With Frank Sinatra's "New York, New York" playing triumphantly in the Bronx, the New York Yankees relish their 2009 world title.

Celebration

Celebration

Baltimore Orioles third baseman Brooks Robinson is flying high after a win in Game 4 of the 1966 World Series.

Oakland A's catcher Gene Tenace emphatically scores the winning run in Game 4 of the 1972 World Series against Cincinnati's "Big Red Machine." The A's went on to win the epic '72 Fall Classic in seven games.

Celebration

38 A's

Celebration

Sandy Koufax (center) is congratulated by
his Los Angeles Dodgers teammates after
Game 7 win in the 1965 Fall Classic.

Photo Credits

MARC LEVINE/NEW YORK METS/MLB PHOTOS: Cover (Citi Field sky); 1; 2–3; 26–27

BRAD MANGIN/MLB PHOTOS: Cover (Tulowitzki); 13; 61; 70–71

COURTESY OF THE TRUSTEES OF THE BOSTON PUBLIC LIBRARY PRINT DEPARTMENT: Cover (Ted Williams); 134

STEPHEN DUNN/GETTY IMAGES: Cover (Rangers celebration); 38–39; 144–145

JONATHAN DANIEL/GETTY IMAGES: Back Cover (White Sox mascot); 29; 37; 130–131

NBLA/MLB PHOTOS: Back Cover (Ty Cobb); 22; 92–93; 117

MLB PHOTOS: Back Cover (Rod Carew); 14–15

MICHAEL ZAGARIS/MLB PHOTOS: 5; 79; 82–83; 135

FRANK HURLEY/NEW YORK DAILY NEWS ARCHIVE/GETTY IMAGES: 6; 108

RICH PILLING/MLB PHOTOS: 8–9; 24–25; 50–51; 55; 58–59; 74–75; 86–87; 106–107; 109; 122–123; 124–125; 125

CHUCK SOLOMON/MLB PHOTOS: 11

BETTMANN/CORBIS: 12

JOHN CORDES/MLB PHOTOS: 16–17; 52

HY PESKIN/SPORTS ILLUSTRATED/GETTY IMAGES: 18–19; 67

JOHN SPRINGER COLLECTION/ CORBIS: 21

MARK CUNNINGHAM/DETROIT TIGERS/MLB PHOTOS: 28; 42–43

JOE GIZA/REUTERS/CORBIS: 31

STEPHEN GREEN/CHICAGO CUBS/MLB PHOTOS: 32–33

RICHARD A. LIPSKI/THE WASHINGTON POST/GETTY IMAGES: 34

ELSA/GETTY IMAGES: 36; 40

DOUG PENSINGER/GETTY IMAGES: 44–45; 80

RON VESELY/MLB PHOTOS: 46; 148; 150–151

RONALD C. MODRA/SPORTS ILLUSTRATED/GETTY IMAGES: 47; 138

JED JACOBSOHN/MLB PHOTOS: 47

MICHAEL IVINS/BOSTON RED SOX/MLB PHOTOS: 48–49

EZRA SHAW/GETTY IMAGES: 53

ROB TRINGALI/ SPORTSCHROME/GETTY IMAGES: 56–57; 136–137

WALTER IOOSS JR./SPORTS ILLUSTRATED/GETTY IMAGES: 62; 66; 88–89; 155; 156–157

CHRISTIAN PETERSEN/GETTY IMAGES: 63; 72–73

JONATHAN WILLEY/ARIZONA DIAMONDBACKS/MLB PHOTOS: 64–65

AL TIELEMANS/SPORTS ILLUSTRATED/GETTY IMAGES: 68; 146

JIM ROGASH/GETTY IMAGES: 69

JED JACOBSOHN/GETTY IMAGES: 76–77

STEPHEN NOWLAND/RICH CLARKSON AND ASSOCIATES, LLC: 81

ROB TRINGALI/MLB PHOTOS: 84; 90–91

ROBERT RIGER/GETTY IMAGES: 94

TOM DIPACE PHOTOGRAPHY: 95

HEINZ KLUETMEIER/ SPORTS ILLUSTRATED/GETTY IMAGES: 96

HERB SCHARFMAN/ SPORTS ILLUSTRATED/GETTY IMAGES: 99

UPI/BETTMANN/CORBIS: 100–101

PHOTO FILE/GETTY IMAGES: 102

GEORGE SILK/TIME LIFE PICTURES/GETTY IMAGES: 104–105

TONY TRIOLO/ SPORTS ILLUSTRATED/GETTY IMAGES: 111

ROGERS PHOTO ARCHIVE/ GETTY IMAGES: 112–113

VINCENT LAFORET/GETTY IMAGES: 114–115

RALPH MORSE/TIME LIFE PICTURES/GETTY IMAGES: 118

RYAN McKEE/RICH CLARKSON AND ASSOCIATES, LLC: 120–121

CHARLIE RIEDEL/AP PHOTO: 126–127

JOHN GRIESHOP/MLB PHOTOS: 128–129

HANK WALKER/TIME LIFE PICTURES/GETTY IMAGES: 133

PHIL GREITZER/NEW YORK DAILY NEWS/GETTY IMAGES: 139

MARC SEROTA/GETTY IMAGES: 140–141

CHUCK SOLOMON/SPORTS ILLUSTRATED/GETTY IMAGES: 142–143

BRUCE KLUCKHOHN/ MINNESOTA TWINS/MLB PHOTOS: 147

BOB DAUGHERTY/AP PHOTO: 152–153

Index

MLB INSIDERS CLUB